Ducati Monster

by Julie Wilson

Acknowledgements

Photographs © Ducati

Copyright © Axis Education 2007

First published in Great Britain by Axis Education Ltd

ISBN 978-1-84618-098-9

Axis Education
PO Box 459
Shrewsbury
SY4 4WZ

Email: enquiries@axiseducation.co.uk

www.axiseducation.co.uk

Printed by The Cromwell Press, Trowbridge, Wiltshire.

This is a Ducati Monster.

It is the Monster 695.

It is a fast motorbike.

The Monster 695.

Ducatis are made in Italy.

The 695 came out in 2006.

It has a lot of power.

It has 73 horsepower.

A powerful bike.

The Monster 695 is comfy to ride.

It has a low seat.

You can put both feet down.

You are in control.

You can put both feet down.

The handlebars are high.

You sit upright.

This bike looks like a Ducati.

It looks good.

It looks good.

The 695 can go as fast as 134 miles per hour.

That is the same as 215 kilometres per hour.

The engine is air-cooled.

This makes it lighter.

The 695 means it has 695cc.

695cc!

The 695 is a neat bike.

It is a good bike for first-timers.

It holds the road well.

Good for first-timers.

A cool design.

The 695 is a neat bike.

This is a Ducati Monster S4Rs.

It is a new model.

It came out in 2006.

The Ducati Monster S4Rs.

This bike is for better riders.

It is a superbike.

It is called a 'street fighter'.

A street fighter.

The S4Rs engine has 130 horsepower.

This makes it good for racing.

It races in the World Superbike Championship.

A good engine for racing.

The S4Rs weighs 177kg.

This is not too heavy.

It is not too light.

Not too heavy ...

The Monster S4Rs has a short wheelbase.

It is 1440mm.

This makes the handling quicker.

... not too light.

The S4Rs' engine has 998cc.

This is a lot of power.

It is a monster of a motor!

998cc!

This bike looks like a racer.

A real monster!

This is the Ducati Super Monster S4Rs.

It is the biggest Monster.

This Monster will make your heart miss a beat!

Watch that heart!

The Super Monster is a bike you dream of.

It has a racing engine.

The Brembo brakes are top class.

It has even got sat nav!

A bike you dream of.

The Super's footrests are smart.

They have been made with care.

They are made of aluminium.

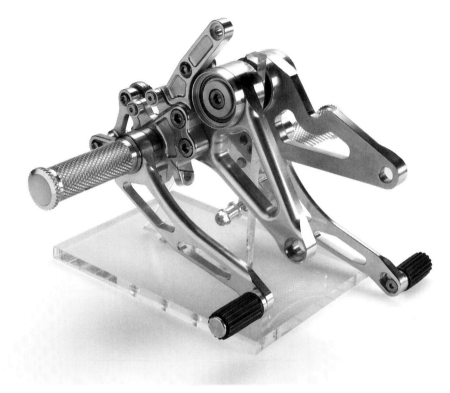

Super footrests.

These Ducatis are full of style.

They turn heads in the street.

They are true monsters!

Want one!

Technical specification – Ducati Monster

Make	Ducati
Model	Monster 695
Engine	695cc
Transmission	6-speed
Frame	Tubular steel
Front tyre	120/60 ZR 17
Exhaust	2 aluminium mufflers
Length	1950mm
Seat height	770mm
Wheelbase	1440mm
Weight	160kg
Fuel tank capacity	14 litres
Maximum power	73hp
Price	£4,995.00

Glossary

air-cooled	cooled with air
aluminium	a type of lightweight metal
Brembo	a type of brake used on cars and motorbikes
capacity	how much petrol the engine can hold
cc (cubic centimetres)	a measure of engine capacity
first-timers	people having a go for the first time
handling	how the bike feels, how it drives
hp	horsepower; a unit of power
kg (kilogram)	a measure of weight (just over two pounds)
litre	a measure of liquid (just under two pints)
maximum	the most, highest
mm (millimetre)	a small measure of length: 10mm = 1cm (centimetre)
neat	cool, smart
rear	the back of the bike
sat nav	a computer unit that tells you which direction to go
footrests	on a motorbike, the parts you put your feet on
transmission	another word for gearbox

upright   straight-backed

wheelbase   the distance between the front and rear wheels